Building Strategic Relationships Through Networking

Networlding Guidebook

Contents

Networlding Overview and Introduction

"Networlding is a long journey rather than a short ride, and you want to make sure that those you share it with are people you truly feel connected to on a deeper level than money. The journey must be marked not only by your continuous success but by the success of others."
—(Networlding p. 37)

WHAT IS NETWORLDING?

Networlding is the science and art of making meaningful connections and leveraging those connections in new and powerful ways. Networlding is an accelerated networking program based on growing mutually beneficial relationships with key connectors who have similar and complementary values.

Networlding is much more effective than traditional networking because it will show you how to create an entire support system that includes both people who will help you in the short term as well as people who will help you leverage long-term, transformational opportunities, time and time again. It also shows you how to create for others and yourself, true fulfillment in the process.

As you read in the opening pages of the text, when Peter Drucker, the guru of management, asked a recent class of MBA students what they would call this new, connected society, they responded, "We'd call it the New Network Society." To take full advantage of this new age, we need to understand how we are all connected and how to use these connections for mutual gain. We also need to make a shift in our professional and personal strategies for getting ahead. This shift is from a "me" perspective to the more leveraged "we" perspective. This means forming and maintaining relationships in radically different ways.

Networlding is the strategy that will allow you to shift your focus from the opportunities, to the people who can help you take advantage of those opportunities . . . to transform relationships from a pipeline to opportunities to a lifeline in our new world of work.

Networlding relationships start when you clearly express your intent in the broad sense of the word. Quickly and convincingly, you communicate your goals and value, and when you do so, people who resonate to your intent will respond. If someone responds positively and you are able to establish a Networlding relationship, you can reap tremendous benefits. Your new partner will not only do more for you in terms of opportunities but in providing an empathetic ear and a source of fresh ideas.

In contrast, **Networking** connections are flimsy because they lack support. When networking, people are bound together because one person needs another to do a deal or create a sale. One particular situation binds them together, and as soon as this situation disintegrates or disappears, there's nothing left of the relationship to keep it strong enough to survive.

NETWORLDING	NETWORKING
Values-based	Goal-based
Leveraged learning	Duplication of efforts
Long-term commitment	Temporary
Relational	Transactional
Conscious, strategic process	Haphazard process
Mutually beneficial	Often one-sided
Systematic	Fragmented
Holistic	Often Materialistic
Intimate	Superficial
Opportunity Expansive	Opportunity Specific
Multi-dimensional	Two-dimensional

The Networlding "Community of Learning & Practice"

In this workshop will be covering all the steps of a seven-step Networlding process. You will be asked to perform exercises for each step of the process. Some of the exercises you will do on your own and others will be done with your group. The seven steps are outlined in the chart below.

STEP NO. OR TITLE	DESCRIPTION
Networlding Overview	Networlding vs. Networking
STEP ONE: Establish a Values-Rich Foundation	Take the Quiz. Identify your top values. Discover linkages to company values and goals.
STEP TWO: Make Connections for Your Primary Circle	Begin completing your Circle profile. Identify who is currently in your Primary Circle and why.
STEP THREE: Expand your Circle	Identify and connect with new people who have similar and complimentary values to build a more complete, leveraged circle.
STEP FOUR: Initiate Exchanging Relationships	Develop relationships more effectively by finding out what matters to others through conscious conversations.
STEP FIVE: Grow and Nurture Relationships	Develop relationships with Primary Circle Partners using The Networlding Support Exchange Model
STEP SIX: Co-create Opportunities	Create transformational opportunities through continuous exchanges
STEP SEVEN: Recreate Your NetWorld and why.	Achieve your goals: constantly reassess and expand relationships that align with your values.
Next Steps and Contract	Contract with yourself to commit to effective Networlding

Guidelines for Effective Networlding Participation

Networlding is about creating communities of support, built on trust, respect and well-being. It is a process of collaboration that achieves mutual goals and leads to professional and personal fulfillment. This is the Age of the Relationship, where our relationships become one of our most critical assets. Networlding is based on a Seven-step process. The following is the commitment I make to this process:

Create a safe Networlding environment and commit to confidentiality so that people can feel safe.

- Contribute to the creation of an environment that supports everyone and gives opportunity for all to participate. I acknowledge that this is not therapy.

- Develop rapport and chemistry first before discussing leads and referrals.

- Be an active listener; listening more than I will talk. Learn about individuals so that you may find ways to support them.

- Be a giver with the intention of giving first and think exchange for mutual benefit.

- Follow-up with those I have met via Networlding to learn more about them and what they care about, to explore what's possible for both of us.

- Return calls promptly.

- Honor values of others and seek to develop relationships with people who share them. (This is a critical time saver.)

- Be considerate of others' time constraints. Include other people in conversations.

- Listen to, support and acknowledge the viewpoints of others and seek to build on what has been said without criticism.

Quality Versus Quantity Self Test

Remember the fable of the tortoise and the hare? The hare was so busy with the quantity of his travels, he paid no attention to the quality of his travels and wound up losing the race. In Networlding, happiness is NOT an over-stuffed Rolodex!

Rate the effectiveness of your current network. Reflect for a moment on the individuals in your current network. Complete the following exercise to assess the current effectiveness of your network.

I. QUANTITY

Rate today's level of activity with your exchanges on a scale of 1-5.
1 being lowest – 5 being highest

1. Attending organization meetings to locate new referral sources

2. Involving yourself in outside activities
    (sports, hobbies religious activities, etc., that involve others)

3. Making calls to new contacts to create referral source relationships

4. Reading articles to identify influencers and potential referral sources in niche markets

5. Asking current contacts to recommend potential referral sources

6. Spending time planning the development of your referral source base.

II. QUALITY

Rate today's level of quality with your exchanges on a scale from 1-5
1 being lowest – 5 being highest

1. Attending organization meetings to locate new referral sources

2. Involving yourself in outside activities
    (sports, hobbies religious activities, etc., that involve others)

3. Making calls to new contacts to create referral source relationships

4. Reading articles to identify influencers and potential referral sources in niche markets.

5. Asking current contacts to recommend potential referral sources

6. Spending time planning the development of your referral source base

If you found your Quality score was lower than your Quantity score, you need to change your focus. A feeling of dissatisfaction can actually be a starting point toward building better Networlding skills. If you take action to improve your current status, it leads to change.

TAKE THE NETWORLDING QUIZ

Questions
Never =1 Seldom =2 Occasionally =3 Often =4 Always =5

1. Believe it is important to make a difference   _____

2. Believe that anything is possible   _____

3. Believe you are guided by strong inner beliefs, intent or principles   _____

4. Believe you create your own rewards   _____

5. Believe you can get anything done through others   _____

6. Believe people are your most creative resource   _____

7. Share your goals with others   _____

8. Build/nurture relationships with those who can help you achieve your goals   _____

9. Limit relationships with selfish individuals and those that don't help you realize your goals _____

10. Respect the creative process and are result/outcome focused   _____

11. Believe that Networlding/Networking shortens the time to get things done   _____

12. Assume that Networlding/Networking is a balanced process of giving and receiving   _____

13. Believe Networlding/Networking can provide all needed resources to reach your goals   _____

14. When Networlding/Networking you ask for what you want   _____

15. When Networlding/Networking you discover others' interests and needs   _____

16. When Networlding/Networking you expect to discover/create new opportunities   _____

17. Networld/Network with influential people who can make things happen   _____

18. Offer emotional, information and other support to your Networld/Network partners   _____

19. Respond quickly to the requests and needs of your Networld/Network partners   _____

20. Measure the results of your Networlding/Networking efforts   _____

Total Your Score   _____
Novice (Score: 20-44), Networker (Score: 45-64), Strategic Networker (Score: 65-84),
Networlding Expert (Score: 85-100)

Four-Level Networlding Matrix

Below is a tool to help you determine your current level of networking effectively.

Level 1 Baseline Networking	Level 2 Qualifying	Level 3 Partnering	Level 4 Collaborating
Joining professional Networking Groups	Attending industry and targeted associations Attending event and identifying a few potential Primary Circle Partners Meeting with current potential Primary Circle Partners you know	Following up by phone and-or email with potential Primary Circle Partners Meeting with new, potential Primary Circle Partners	Cross-selling, identifying potential strategic alliance partners
Attending general conferences and tradeshows	Attending events with targeted influencers in attendance	Building agreement with Primary Circle Partners to formalize a partnership	Creating strategic alliances internally and externally
Participating in civic, non-profit events (e.g. fundraisers)	Targeting specific organizations of value Joining boards and committees	Scheduling meetings with Primary Circle Partners	Building new business ventures with Partners
Networking with friends, family and relatives, as well as people you meet in your daily work or social life	Participating in leadership roles (ambassadorship), etc.	Leveraging relationships Actively participating in helping targeted organizations and Primary Circle Partners achieve goals Working all levels of the Support Exchange Model Meeting at least monthly with Primary Circle Partners	

STEP 1: Establish a Values-Rich Foundation

"Try not to be a man of success, but rather a man of value."—Albert Einstein

Before you can become well networked and collaborative you need to identify your top values. These values live with you daily. They drive your behavior in the workplace and most of all they will help build a powerful network of people who hold similar and complementary values. These like-valued people will become your partners on the path to transformational opportunities.

From the guidebook: Chapters 1, 2 & 3
1. Networlding, Chapter 1, "What is Networlding, Anyway?" (pp. 1-23) and Chapter 2, "Networlding Golden Rules" (pp. 24-36). Use the book as a resource during your Networlding journey.

2. Networlding, Chapter 3, "Step One: Establish a Values-Rich Foundation," (pp. 37-53).

EXERCISE A:
IDENTIFY YOUR TOP VALUES

Values are the principles that guide your actions on a daily basis. Becoming strongly aware of your values and creating goals that reflect those values builds a foundation for success. Living your personal and work lives according to those values creates a feeling of authenticity in the way you present yourself. Authenticity inspires trust and confidence and leads to credibility.

Values clarification is both the first and final step in laying that foundation for success. If you understand what is important to you and what drives you, you can align your work to your values and increase your level of passion and satisfaction in your life and work.

Values clarification is also an imperative step in the transition from doing the things you are skilled at to doing the things you are passionate about. You can be competent without being passionate about a job, project or task. When you identify an overlap between what motivates you and where you excel, you've found a passion!

You'll know a job, project or task is a passion when it's easy, fun and time slips away because you are totally engaged!

You are at your most productive when you are passionate about a job or task You are better able to achieve your goals and objectives when you are engaged in tasks about which they are passionate.

Achieving a top level of performance begins with you. As you identify the things that are important to you and find your passions you create an environment that facilitates success. The first step is in this process is identifying your values.

In this exercise, you will identify and clarify your values. Once you establish your values and set your goals, you can then translate your goals into actions.

VALUES LIST

The following table lists many personal values, but is in no way intended to be complete.
Feel free to use these, or add any others important to you, as you complete your pre-work.

Exercise: Check off as many values as apply to you for today

Achievement	Advancement	Adventure
Affiliation	Authority	Autonomy
Balance	Collaboration	Community
Competence	Competition	Connection
Contribution	Cooperation	Courage
Creativity	Economic prosperity	Economic security
Empowerment	Fame	Family
Focus	Freedom	Friendship
Fun	Giver	Happiness
Health	Helpfulness	Honoring
Inner Harmony	Integrity	Involvement
Knowing	Knowledge	Loyalty
Making a Difference	Non-judgment	Order
Trust	Personal	Development
Pleasure	Power	Quality
Recognition	Responsibility	Safety
Self Motivation	Self respect	Service
Spirituality	Success	Wisdom

Note: All of the values listed are important. You are identifying what drives you. For example, do not feel compelled to select "family" as a value if it is not what motivates you to action. That does not mean you don't care for your family.

List below your top four values (in order of priority if possible):

1.

2.

3.

4.

STRATEGIES FOR LEVERAGING YOUR VALUES

- Remember, nothing is etched in stone. Your values may change over time. Different values will be more important to you at various stages of your life.

  There may be different values for you in the various business markets, industries, company targets and geographic considerations that go into growing your business or developing your career.

- Did your values align with your current work? What needs to change?

- Think about your work for the past few years. What were you doing when your values were honored? When did your work conflict with your values?

GOAL CREATION

Create a corresponding goal that aligns with your values for the next 60 days. Make sure your goals are S.M.A.R.T.: Specific, Measurable, and Attainable, Results oriented and Time-bound. Write it on the worksheet on the following page. Share your goal and discuss which of your top 4 values apply. What strategies will you employ to achieve that goal? Write it down on the next page.

VALUES, GOALS AND STRATEGY ALIGNMENT WORKSHEET:

Values

Goal

Strategies

1.

2.

3.

4.

For example, say your target industry is healthcare and you choose as one of your top goals to secure a new key relationship. Let's also say that one of your top values is creativity. How can you use your value of creativity to help you achieve your goal? One strategy might be to find one key prospect you have been in contact with and set up a brainstorming meeting with them to see how you might partner to create a viable business opportunity for you in that sector. An executive in a web development firm tried this approach and found that he was able to eliminate going through an RFP (request-for-proposal) process.

Next steps: Share your values with a couple of people who know you very well (e.g. colleague, spouse, friend, etc.) Ask them to identify what they believe are your top values.

Are you surprised at the responses? Many people have found that the values you think you exhibit daily are actually not evident, often times even to those long time.

INSIGHTS: Take a few minutes to capture insights you gained having gone through this step.

STEP 2: Make Connections For Your Primary Circle

"Just ask yourself: To whom would I turn to get something done—someone who is strongly connected to two people or someone who is lightly connected to 150 people? Any doubts about your answer?"—James M. Kouzes, Author, *The Leadership Challenge*

In today's fast-paced environment you need to be able to thrive in changing market conditions. Like many people you may also want to find work that is both fun and financially rewarding. To accomplish this you need to build networks or "Circles" that will leverage both your skills and interests. Step Two in the Networlding process involves the formation of your Primary Circle, a group of no more than five people, to start with, who hold complimentary values to yours and are ready, willing and able to start the process of Networlding with you.

EXERCISE A:
CREATE YOUR PRIMARY CIRCLE

Identify potential members of your Primary Circle—people you already know and then narrow down the list of potential members by assessing how each potential member's values would fit with your own. You will partner with a member of your learning Circle to facilitate forming your Primary Circle.

Use the guide on page 15 to fill in the names of people you know who work in the following fields:

Social Networking Leaders	Assoc. Membership Directors	Trade Assoc. Directors	Past bosses	Clients or customers
Non-Profit Heads	Insurance agents/ financial planners	Government officials	Speakers	Colleagues
Restaurant Owners	Librarian	Chamber executives	Editors of professional journals	People who support the causes I care about
Religious leaders	Colleagues who have moved to new jobs	IT consultants	Friends	People who work in complementary businesses to mine
Bankers	Doctors	Board members Alumni	Colleagues from past employers	
				College friends
Relatives	Accountant	Customers/Clients	Neighbors	
Lawyer	Teachers/ Professors	Publishers	Real estate agent	
				Check off those

people on your list, above, whose values complement your own. Review pages 58-62 in Networlding. Additionally, use the list, below, to help select your primary circle partners.

CHARACTERISTICS OF GREAT MEMBERS OF A PRIMARY CIRCLE

1. Has a wide variety of connections
2. Is very observant of people and environments
3. Has a talent for staying in touch
4. Outwardly focused
5. Sensitive to other's needs
6. Has access to different types of information
7. Has a natural talent for connection and helping
8. Focused on diversity
9. Spiritually, intellectually and emotionally balanced
10. Is an influencer to a broad base

13

Cull your Circle down to no more than five people by asking who may be ready, willing and able to Networld with you over the course of the next two months.

Ready
Do they have the time to meet with you, preferably every other week, for the next two months?

Willing
Can they commit to these meetings and/or conversations?

Able
Do they feel and/or think they have something to contribute (connections, ideas, etc)?

Even one person is sufficient to begin Networlding effectively. List your five potential **Primary Circle** partners, below:

1.

2.

3.

4.

5.

EXERCISE B:
FURTHER DISCERNING GOOD PRIMARY CIRCLE PARTNERS

At your meeting or through a conversation with each potential partner, following are examples of talking points to use to discern whether you will have a viable Circle partner:

- Your respective interests in being in one another's Primary Circle.

- The Networlding process as you have experienced it so far.

- Your top values and their connection to your goal and strategies for achieving your goal.

- A commitment by both of you to meet at least once a month (preferably twice a month) for the next two months to have Networlding exchanges (presented in Step 5 of Networlding.)

It's best to prepare and design specific, and tailored targeted questions for each partner that will help both of you decide the best way to proceed in building a successful partnership.

INSIGHTS: Take a few minutes to capture insights you gained having gone through this step.

STEP 3: Expand Your Circles

"Reality lies in how you see things."—Pablo Picasso

Once you have reviewed your current network and identified five or fewer key connections for your Primary Circle, you can begin to fill in the gaps in your Circle so that you have a rich, divergent base of connections that will help pursue your business connections. Vendors, partners, existing customers, people in other divisions—anyone who is important to achieving your goals, should be considered.

Growing your Primary Circle is a fun, exciting process that, even with a little effort, will yield great results for you.

From the guidebook: Chapter 5
Networlding, Chapter 5, "Step 3: Expand Your Circles," (pp. 70-101) as a complement to the Networlding process.

EXERCISE A:
FIGURE OUT WHO ARE POTENTIAL PARTNERS

In this exercise, you will focus on the expansion of your Primary Circle. You will begin by reflecting on your reading from the book and developing a description of those people who would be good partners for you to exchange.

POTENTIAL PARTNER GUIDE
First, think about your values; think about the 5 potential members of your primary Circle from the last exercise; imagine the ideal mix of people you would want. Avoid editing yourself; let your ideas and imagination flow. Jot down your wish list on Potential Partner Guide (below.)
Explore sources to find connectors, influencers. . . in other words, Networlders.

Consider the following:

- FAST Company magazine

- 40 under 40 lists (Crains usually publishes this)

- Magazine that list the best companies for women to work in, the best ethical companies, the companies with the best CEO's (Sources include: Forbes, Crains, Fortune, Inc.etc)

- Best Companies for Women to Work For?

- Showcased articles in local newspapers—business sections, on top business leaders (you are looking for people who, through their words or stories, espouse complimentary values to yours.)

- Referrals from your current Networlding partners. Do this by asking, "What one person do you know what is the best value-based networker, leader, influencer, mentor, etc?"

- Referrals from your local chamber to top business leaders.

- Research on the web with headings such as "socially responsible companies, business leaders, top business leaders, etc.)

Write down the names of up to 10 people with what you believe would be their top values.

1.

2.

3.

4.

5.

6.

7.

8.

9.

10.

EXERCISE B:
CULL YOUR EXPANDED CIRCLE DOWN TO NO MORE THAN FIVE PEOPLE

Remember, Networlding is about quality versus quantity. During this step, you need to focus on adding five or fewer people to your Primary Circle. Take twenty minutes and go through each of your selected potential partners and ask yourself the following three questions:

1. Which of these potential partners might be ready, willing and able (as you did in Step #2) to work with you currently?

2. Which five people would be the best Complementors in helping you achieve your current goal (e.g. who is geographically, conveniently located, who is someone you can more easily reach, etc.)?

3. Who in my current network can I speak with to gain an introduction to one of these people or to someone else who might be able to introduce me to one of these people (e.g. Six degrees of Connection.)

Your Culled Circle of Five Primary Circle Partners

1.

2.

3.

4.

5.

INSIGHTS: Take a few minutes to capture insights you gained having gone through this step.

STEP 4: Initiate Exchanging Relationships

"See things as you would have them be, instead of as they are." —Robert Collier

Now that you have continued to develop your Primary Circle, it's time to prepare for ongoing conversations that lead to discovering new opportunities for yourself and your Networlding partner. Initiating exchanging relationships is a critical skill in today's connected society where you will need to form quick, meaningful relationships with people with whom you will partner for emerging market opportunities.

From the guidebook: Chapter 6
Networlding, Chapter 6, "Step 4: Initiate Exchanging Relationships," (pp. 102-126).

AGENDA

Review and discuss your pre-meeting exercises with your learning circle.

- How difficult or easy was it to identify new people for your Primary Networlding Circle?

- What would have made this process easier?

- How did you use your values to identify new Networlding partners.

Networlding really works when you learn to initiate relationships that help both you and your prospective Networlding partners get into an exchange. This means focusing the conversation around things you have in common and ways you can support one another. The following is an exercise to help you develop this skill.

EXERCISE A:
FILL OUT YOUR NETWORLDING PROFILE

Filling your profile will help you solidify in your mind those things that are of importance as well as what you need to communicate to others with whom you want to connect. This tool has been one of the most effective tools for Networlding participants. You will also use a similar tool to create profiles for members of your primary circle in Step 5.

YOUR NETWORLDING PROFILE

Name: Primary Phone:

Primary Email:

Employed [ ]   Self-employed [ ]   Industry: Title: Employed By:

Current or Former Company's Products and/or Services – Sound Bite:
A quick 30-second overview that defines what you do and how you can help others.

Personal Professional Skills & Responsibilities – Personal Values:
What you value most in your personal and work relationships?

Personal Information Affecting Future Decisions – Personal Interests:
What you do you for fun?

Supporting Others in Networlding – Help Others Connect:
How you can help connect people to those they want to meet or create the opportunities they want to create?

The kinds of people or opportunities to be connected with – How would you like others to help or support you:
Think about the next 30-60 days as a focus on the support you need.

Your last great Networlding opportunity you created – The story about how you connected with someone and worked on an opportunity together: **Networlders who share stories about clients, prospects, referral sources, etc., helps others and helps you with more connections.**

21

EXERCISE B:
INITIATE A NETWORLDING SUPPORT EXCHANGE

Use the Networlding Support Exchange Model (below) to start the process of building effective relationships. An effective conversation with someone you are just meeting starts with questions that speak to the interests and needs of the person with whom you are speaking. Finding out, first, what matters currently to someone you are talking with and second, working a conversation around what matters to them and to you, will grow a strong and lasting foundation for ongoing exchanges. Therefore, a certain amount of practice will make a big difference.

Review the seven different levels of support exchanges, adding additional questions and support comments around each level of support. If you have support exchange cards, use them for this exercise.

SUPPORT EXCHANGE MODEL

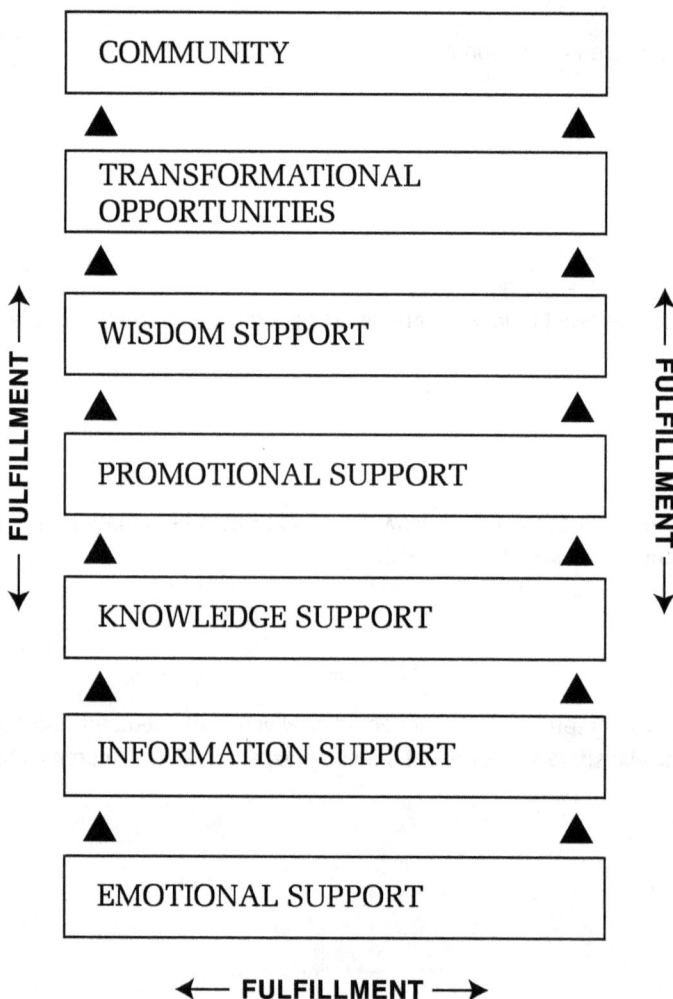

```
                    ┌─────────────────────────────┐
                    │  COMMUNITY                  │
                    └─────────────────────────────┘
                       ▲                     ▲
                    ┌─────────────────────────────┐
                    │  TRANSFORMATIONAL           │
                    │  OPPORTUNITIES              │
                    └─────────────────────────────┘
                       ▲                     ▲
  ↑                 ┌─────────────────────────────┐                 ↑
  │                 │  WISDOM SUPPORT             │                 │
  FULFILLMENT       └─────────────────────────────┘       FULFILLMENT
  │                    ▲                     ▲                 │
  ↓                 ┌─────────────────────────────┐                 ↓
                    │  PROMOTIONAL SUPPORT        │
                    └─────────────────────────────┘
                       ▲                     ▲
                    ┌─────────────────────────────┐
                    │  KNOWLEDGE SUPPORT          │
                    └─────────────────────────────┘
                       ▲                     ▲
                    ┌─────────────────────────────┐
                    │  INFORMATION SUPPORT        │
                    └─────────────────────────────┘
                       ▲                     ▲
                    ┌─────────────────────────────┐
                    │  EMOTIONAL SUPPORT          │
                    └─────────────────────────────┘
```

← FULFILLMENT →

EMOTIONAL SUPPORT EXCHANGE – QUESTIONS

- "What brought you here today (tonight, etc.)?"
- "What is going on in your professional life right now that really excites you?"
- "What one project are you working on that is most interesting?"
- "What is it about this organization that you like most?"
- "What other groups are you involved with that you really like?"
- (For people out of work) "What type of job are you looking for that would be even better than the one you currently left?" "What about your old job made you the happiest?" "What's the most emotionally satisfying project that you have worked on?"

EMOTIONAL SUPPORT EXCHANGE – EXPRESSIONS OF SUPPORT

Examples:

- "You are a good listener."
- "You have good insight(s) into my challenges."
- "You offer me a way to see things differently."
- "You are well versed in your field."
- "You share great ideas."

Your Turn:

INFORMATIONAL SUPPORT EXCHANGE – QUESTIONS

Examples:

- "What's the last good business book you read?"
- "What types of organizations are you interested in getting involved with (size, travel involved, industry, work environment, salary)?"
- "What industries are you most interested in?"
- "What kind of information would you like on specific businesses?
- "What is one of the best ideas you learned in business recently?"
- "What are a few of the best information resources you have found?"

Your Turn:

INFORMATIONAL SUPPORT EXCHANGE – EXPRESSIONS OF SUPPORT

Examples:

- "I have some useful information on your area of interest. I will email it to you."
- "I know of a good organization for you to explore possible membership."
- "I know an industry leader who I have heard of (read about, etc.)"
  His or her name is _____ and this is what I know about her or him.
- "_____ (someone I know) may have useful information that would be of value to you."
- "There is an upcoming seminar on the subject you are interested in. I will get you information on it and email you."
- "I just read an article that is exactly about the point you just made. Let me send it to you."

Your Turn:

KNOWLEDGE SUPPORT EXCHANGE – QUESTIONS

Examples:

- "What three ways could my clients (or customers) benefit from your services?"
- "What area of expertise don't you have that you would like to get more experience in?"
- "What's one area you would like to develop that you are not currently developing?"
- "What's is most exciting about your experience in your area of expertise?"
- "What is new in your field that others might not know?"

Your Turn:

KNOWLEDGE SUPPORT EXCHANGE – EXPRESSIONS OF SUPPORT

Examples:

- "My experience in _____ might be useful in addressing your current challenges."
- "I have learned to draft a great proposal. I would be happy to share help you with one you are working on."
- "I have talked with a number of experts on the subject you are interested in. I would be happy to share my insights."
- "I have done research on your industry. I can share what I have discovered."
- "I have experience with the process you are working on optimizing that I can share."

Your Turn:

PROMOTIONAL SUPPORT EXCHANGE – QUESTIONS

Examples:

- "What are your top three strengths that you would like others to know about?"
- "What would you like people to say about you?"
- "What have past clients or business partners said is unique about you?"
- "Which of your last, few, successful projects were the most exciting?"
- "Which two people would like to have know more about you?
- "What three or four organizations would you like to know more about you and your work?"

Your Turn:

PROMOTIONAL SUPPORT EXCHANGE – EXPRESSIONS OF SUPPORT

Examples:

- "I will mention your name to others I meet this next week and let them know more about the things your are doing."
- "I will share your strengths with a couple of colleagues who might benefit from them."
- "I am going to tell all my friends about your business."
- "I am going to make sure I tell as many people as I can regularly about you."
- "I am going to write about you in my next newsletter, column, etc."
- "I will tell my board about you and your organization."

Your Turn:

WISDOM SUPPORT EXCHANGE – QUESTIONS

Examples:
- "What's one of the most important things you have accomplished in your professional life so far?"
- "What is a top piece of wisdom you regularly impart to others?"
- "What's one of the wisest things you have heard someone else say?"
- "Who said it?"
- "Who is a wise person you admire a great deal in history/business? Why?"

Your Turn:

WISDOM SUPPORT EXCHANGE – EXPRESSIONS OF SUPPORT

Examples:
- "I know after 15 years of experience that what you are proposing is right on."
- "My experience of 10 years says I would recommend you to/for

  _____."
- "My experience tells me not to do what you are proposing and I have a better idea."
- "I have found what you want to do just won't work, but I can tell you what will."
- "You can ask me for help with your project for I have done years of work in that area."
- "You are very wise in your plan for your career (or business). I say this because _____."

Your Turn:

TRANSFORMATIONAL OPPORTUNITIES SUPPORT EXCHANGE –
QUESTIONS

Examples:

- "What is a 'pie-in-the sky' wish for you? How might this become a reality?"
- "What transformational outcome did you take part in or lead?"
- "What transformational outcome did you not participate in, but wish you did? Why?"
- "What one thing haven't you done yet in your career that you wish you could do right now?"
- "If you were to have the most successful year you have ever had, what would have happened?"
- "What three people do you think are transformational leaders and why?"
- "What three people would you like to work with on a transformational opportunity and why?"

Your Turn:

TRANSFORMATIONAL OPPORTUNITIES SUPPORT EXCHANGE –
EXPRESSIONS OF SUPPORT

Examples:

- "Let's partner together. At least let's explore that."
- "Let's write a book (article) together."
- "I think you should create an audio tape of what you do best and I'll help you. Perhaps you can do the same for me."
- "I have the perfect project for you (or for us.)"
- "Let's create a seminar together."
- "Let's co-sponsor a roundtable (or workshop) for our clients or customers."

Your Turn:

COMMUNITY SUPPORT EXCHANGE – QUESTIONS

Examples:

- "What three charities or non-profits do you admire the most and why?"
- "What one project have you completed that could now be leveraged out to support your community?"
- "What is one of the most pressing needs within your community that you have passion or desire to get involved in?"
- "What is one of the most exciting stories about a non-profit or community initiative that you participated in?"
- "Who are three people you admire who exemplify community leadership? What types of projects have they led?"

Your Turn:

COMMUNITY SUPPORT EXCHANGE – EXPRESSIONS OF SUPPORT

Examples:

- "When we finish this project not only will these people benefit but their children will benefit as well."
- "This product not only benefits this company's shareholders, it also makes a difference for the whole community."
- "The company will benefit with this product and so will the environment."
- "This project will impact schools and government as well as business."

Your Turn:

COMMUNITY SUPPORT EXCHANGE - OUR TIME

EXERCISE B:
**PARTNER WITH A LEARNING CIRCLE PARTICIPANT AND CONDUCT
A SUPPORT EXCHANGE CONVERSATION.**

EXERCISE C:
**CREATE POWERFUL RELATIONSHIPS THROUGH CONSCIOUS
CONVERSATIONS.**

Share your observations and impressions from this exercise.

BONUS 1: **EXTRA GREAT QUESTIONS**

Ask questions that help others create value-based success stories.

- Who is one of the influential people you've had some kind of relationship with?
- What is one of the best pieces of advice you have ever had?
- Who gave it to you?
- Who is one of the most fun professional executives you have ever worked with?
- Which of your co-workers have you most admired?
- What project or initiative are you most excited about currently?
- Who is the most empowering boss you have every worked with?
- What have they done to empower you?
- What is your proudest achievement on an accomplishment of a project you partnered on?

INSIGHTS: Take a few minutes to capture insights you gained having gone through this step.

STEP 5: Grow and Nurture Relationships
Maintain And Deepen Existing Relationships

"Ah, that a man's reach should exceed his grasp, or what's a heaven for."—Robert Browning

You have created your values foundation, aligned your goals with your values, attached your values to action strategies and identified Networlding partnerships with existing and potential Primary Circle Partners. Now you will leverage your Primary Circle to grow transformational opportunities for yourself and your partners. Having regular conversations with your partners does this. Having a goal aligned with your value(s) and associated with value statements makes conscious conversations rich with your experiences, skills and talents to form a map.

From the guidebook: Chapter 7
1. Networlding, Chapter 7, " Step 5: Grow and Nurture Relationships" (pp. 127-148) as a complement to the Networlding process.

EXERCISE A:
CREATE YOUR VALUE PROPOSITION FOR NETWORLDING EXCHANGES

In this exercise you will focus on building an ongoing exchange to help you achieve your current goal and the goals of your Networlding partners. You will also develop value proposition statement to help your partners understand the unique strengths and experiences you bring to a Networlding Exchange that will help you achieve your goal and enable them to promote you to new connections.

For example, your personal accomplishments and results; your ability to serve as an exemplar; a client's/employer's intrinsic trust in you; your credibility; the sense of unity, direction and purpose that you can provide; your perspective from other companies/industries; the reference point you create, which will be an ongoing focus; the skills you can impart; your singular knowledge or approaches; talents you bring to bear in delivery, or your reputation in the field.

Two people with a similar goal and complementary values will have different VP statements because of the skills and experiences they bring to relationships.

EXERCISE B:
IDENTIFY YOUR VALUE PROPOSITION STATEMENTS

Write your unique VP (value propositions) in the chart listed below, one in each box.

VALUE PROPOSITIONS

Example: At Networlding our unique value proposition is that we focus on value-based networking.	Example: Our edge is that we accelerate goal achievement.	Example: Our strength lies in our twenty years helping Fortune 500 companies maximize the potential of their networks both inside and outside the organization.

EXERCISE C:
LINK YOUR GOAL TO YOUR VALUE PROPOSITION STATEMENT

Write your goal in the space provided below. List the support you will request from your Primary Circle Partners and identify who you will make the request of and what you can offer in exchange (using the Support Exchange Model as a tool)?

My Goal	What is the support I will request from my Primary Circle Partners?	Current partners who can help me achieve my goal and what exchange can I propose?
Example: Bring in two new clients	Example: I would like an introduction to a top executive at a Fortune 1000 organizations.	Meeting with Jane to discuss her connection at targeted companies and, in turn, ask Jane what type of support I can help her with.

EXERCISE D:
PRESENT YOUR GOAL AND VALUE PROPOSITION STATEMENT

- Share, using the Support Exchange Model as a guide.
- Note the value propositions you bring to take your relationships to a deeper level.
- Explore and talk about things you will share that you have in common—similar/complementary values.
- Discuss potential mutual opportunities you have.
- Ask your Circle partner to share the same.
- Make plans for another conversation within the next week.

EXERCISE E:
DEEPEN YOUR RELATIONSHIPS THROUGH CONVERSATIONS

Think about your goal, value propositions and feedback from others. What were the highlights of your last exchange that you will use to **leverage relationships** in the development of your Primary Circle?

Use the Support Exchange Conversation

Use the "Awareness, Recognition, Ownership, Leverage" paradigm below

Questions to Ask Primary Circle Participants:

Ready	Do they have the time?
Willing	Can they commit to conversations once a month at least for an hour?
Able	Do they think they have something to contribute to you? Do you think you have something to contribute to them? At every level of the Support Exchange Model use the sample questions to identify areas of support you can offer one another.

Your shared goal is to move from **awareness** of one another's interests and needs to **recognition** that you can indeed support one another to an actual **ownership** of those needs to the point of **leverage** where you use all levels of the support exchange model to fulfill one another's goals.

Awareness   **Recognition**   **Ownership**   **Leverage**

INSIGHTS: Take a few minutes to capture insights you gained having gone through this step.

35

STEP 6: Co-Create Opportunities

"Do not dismiss any encounter as insignificant." —John Header, The Tao of Leadership

How can you best create transformational opportunities? Sometimes you're so focused on your day-to-day obligations that you fail to take the time to create, or co-create with your Networlding partners, opportunities that could benefit you and your organization in powerful, unique ways. You can achieve your goals much faster if you use your Networlding partnerships as brain trusts. In addition, your partners can help you find things you didn't know existed, and enable you to avoid roadblocks and obstacles to success.

From the guidebook: Chapter 8
1.Networlding, Chapter 8, "Step 6: Co-create Opportunities," (pp. 149-170).

EXERCISE A:
DEVELOPING AN OPPORTUNITY

Group Discussion – Starting Exchanges and Supporting Each Other
In your group, discuss the following questions and capture insights below. Identify someone to present your insights to the total group.

- How do you start your exchange(s) with your Networlding partner(s)?

- How do you develop trust?
  For example, what things do you offer for support?What do your Networlding partner(s) offer?

- What obstacles do you see stopping you from having a successful exchange?

- How can you support your other team player's perceived obstacles (role playing, attending networking events together, etc.)?

- What best practices can you and your group identify that will help build better relationships with Networlding partners?

EXERCISE B:
CO-CREATION OPPORTUNITY QUESTIONS

In this exercise partner with one person in your Learning Circle and have a conversation designed to find ways to help one another achieve your goals and even co-create opportunities. Refer to your Goal and Value Proposition Statements in Step 5.

Answers to the following questions leads to co-creation opportunities.

1. **What are the greatest challenges/trends impacting your (our), if relevant, profession today?**

2. **In the next year, what are the greatest opportunities you have for growth?**

3. What can we do for one another within the next couple of weeks
   that will help each of us move closer to realizing our goals?

4. Share information on one project or account opportunity you are
   currently working on and ask for new ideas to better succeed.
   Think about and record this cutting-edge information.

5. **Is there a way to create a co-opportunity here?**

INSIGHTS: Take a few minutes to capture insights you gained having gone through this step.

STEP 7: Recreate Your Networld

"If we think we can do it on our own today, we are sadly mistaken."
—Jack Welch

Step seven is really about the constant reassessment of your Networld. This practice will make Net-worlding a part of your everyday life—both at work and outside of work. Additional coaching of the process, which is what you are about to experience, will help you make Networlding a highly conscious competence, helping you leverage your ability to communicate ideas quickly and effectively. You and your organization will benefit from your ability to quickly get your ideas communicated with others allowing for rapid deployment of strategies critical to organizational success. In the process you will find yourself living a happier, balanced life where your ideas are listened to and understood. In other words, you become a true player in The New Network Economy.

From the guidebook: Chapters 9 & 10
1. Networlding, Chapter 9, " Step 7: Re-create Your Networld" (pp. 171-190) and Chapter 10, "Thriving in the Networlding Universe" (pp. 191-202) as a complement to the Networlding process.

EXERCISE A:
RE-CREATING YOUR NETWORLD

Making the Process Easier

1. Discuss your experiences and wisdom gained since the last step.

- How difficult or easy do you think it will be to recreate your Networld?
- How can you use your values to recreate your Networld?
- What best practice can you identify to recreate your Networld?

TAKE THE NETWORLDING QUIZ AGAIN

Never =1   Seldom=2   Occasionally=3   Often=4   Always=5

1. Believe it is important to make a difference   _____

2. Believe that anything is possible   _____

3. Believe you are guided by strong inner beliefs, intent or principles   _____

4. Believe you create your own rewards   _____

5. Believe you can get anything done through others   _____

6. Believe people are your most creative resource   _____

7. Share your goals with others   _____

8. Build/nurture relationships with those who can help you achieve your goals   _____

9. Limit relationships with selfish individuals and those that don't help you realize your goals   _____

10. Respect the creative process and are result/outcome focused   _____

11. Believe that Networlding/Networking shortens the time to get things done   _____

12. Assume that Networlding/Networking is a balanced process of giving and receiving   _____

13. Believe Networlding/Networking can provide all needed resources to reach your goals   _____

14. When Networlding/Networking you ask for what you want   _____

15. When Networlding/Networking you discover others' interests and needs   _____

16. When Networlding/Networking you expect to discover/create new opportunities   _____

17. Networld/Network with influential people who can make things happen   _____

18. Offer emotional, information and other support to your Networld/Network partners   _____

19. Respond quickly to the requests and needs of your Networld/ Network partners   _____

20. Measure the results of your Networlding/Networking efforts   _____

Total Your Score Now   _____

Total Your Score At Start

Novice (Score: 20-44), Networker (Score: 45-64), Strategic Networker (Score: 65-84), Networlding Expert (Score: 85-100)

EXERCISE B:
REVIEWING YOUR COMMITMENT TO THE NETWORLDING PROCESS.

In this final set of exercise, you will review your learning and results from the previous six steps. A key element of these exercises is adding your learnings to your collective knowledge base. You will do this by creating a summary of your success stories and best practices to be turned in at the group meeting.

Review your notes at the end of each step and identify key lessons.
Make notes here:

What new business opportunities have you generated at the completion of this course? Make notes here:

Discuss what more you can do to support your Primary Circle partners' goals to achieve success and what further support you can ask for to achieve your goals.

List the actions you will take to apply the Networlding Steps into your day-to-day activities and get better business faster.

List any anticipated roadblocks to your success and steps to overcome them.

YOUR NETWORLDING PRIMARY CIRCLE PARTNER PROFILE
(Use 1 per circle partner)

Name: Primary Phone: Primary Email:

Employed [ ]   Self-employed [ ]   Industry   Title   Employed By:

Current or Former Company's Products and/or Services – Sound Bite: (A quick 30-second overview that defines what you do and how you can help others.)

Personal Professional Skills & Responsibilities – Personal Values: (What you value most in your personal and work relationships?)

Personal Information Affecting Future Decisions – Personal Interests: (What you do you for fun?)

Supporting Others in Networlding – Help Others Connect: (How you can help connect people to those they want to meet or create the opportunities they want to create?)

The kinds of people or opportunities to be connected with – How would you like others to help or support you: (Think about the next 30-60 days as a focus on the support you need.)

Your last great Networlding opportunity you created – The story about how you connected with someone and worked on an opportunity together: (Networlders who share stories about clients, prospects, referral sources, etc., helps others and helps you with more connections.)

YOUR NETWORLDING PRIMARY CIRCLE PARTNER PROFILE

(Use 1 per circle partner)

Name: Primary Phone: Primary Email:

Employed [ ]   Self-employed [ ]   Industry   Title   Employed By:

Current or Former Company's Products and/or Services – Sound Bite: (A quick 30-second overview that defines what you do and how you can help others.)

Personal Professional Skills & Responsibilities – Personal Values: (What you value most in your personal and work relationships?)

Personal Information Affecting Future Decisions – Personal Interests: (What you do you for fun?)

Supporting Others in Networlding – Help Others Connect: (How you can help connect people to those they want to meet or create the opportunities they want to create?)

The kinds of people or opportunities to be connected with – How would you like others to help or support you: (Think about the next 30-60 days as a focus on the support you need.)

Your last great Networlding opportunity you created – The story about how you connected with someone and worked on an opportunity together: (Networlders who share stories about clients, prospects, referral sources, etc., helps others and helps you with more connections.)

45

YOUR NETWORLDING PRIMARY CIRCLE PARTNER PROFILE

(Use 1 per circle partner)

Name: Primary Phone: Primary Email:

Employed [ ]   Self-employed [ ]   Industry   Title   Employed By:

Current or Former Company's Products and/or Services – Sound Bite: (A quick 30-second overview that defines what you do and how you can help others.)

Personal Professional Skills & Responsibilities – Personal Values: (What you value most in your personal and work relationships?)

Personal Information Affecting Future Decisions – Personal Interests: (What you do you for fun?)

Supporting Others in Networlding – Help Others Connect: (How you can help connect people to those they want to meet or create the opportunities they want to create?)

The kinds of people or opportunities to be connected with – How would you like others to help or support you: (Think about the next 30-60 days as a focus on the support you need.)

Your last great Networlding opportunity you created – The story about how you connected with someone and worked on an opportunity together: (Networlders who share stories about clients, prospects, referral sources, etc., helps others and helps you with more connections.)

YOUR NETWORLDING PRIMARY CIRCLE PARTNER PROFILE

(Use 1 per circle partner)

Name: Primary Phone: Primary Email:

Employed [ ]   Self-employed [ ]   Industry   Title   Employed By:

Current or Former Company's Products and/or Services – Sound Bite: (A quick 30-second overview that defines what you do and how you can help others.)

Personal Professional Skills & Responsibilities – Personal Values: (What you value most in your personal and work relationships?)

Personal Information Affecting Future Decisions – Personal Interests: (What you do you for fun?)

Supporting Others in Networlding – Help Others Connect: (How you can help connect people to those they want to meet or create the opportunities they want to create?)

The kinds of people or opportunities to be connected with – How would you like others to help or support you: (Think about the next 30-60 days as a focus on the support you need.)

Your last great Networlding opportunity you created – The story about how you connected with someone and worked on an opportunity together: (Networlders who share stories about clients, prospects, referral sources, etc., helps others and helps you with more connections.)

47

YOUR NETWORLDING PRIMARY CIRCLE PARTNER PROFILE
(Use 1 per circle partner)

Name: Primary Phone: Primary Email:

Employed [ ]   Self-employed [ ]   Industry   Title   Employed By:

Current or Former Company's Products and/or Services – Sound Bite: (A quick 30-second overview that defines what you do and how you can help others.)

Personal Professional Skills & Responsibilities – Personal Values: (What you value most in your personal and work relationships?)

Personal Information Affecting Future Decisions – Personal Interests: (What you do you for fun?)

Supporting Others in Networlding – Help Others Connect: (How you can help connect people to those they want to meet or create the opportunities they want to create?)

The kinds of people or opportunities to be connected with – How would you like others to help or support you: (Think about the next 30-60 days as a focus on the support you need.)

Your last great Networlding opportunity you created – The story about how you connected with someone and worked on an opportunity together: (Networlders who share stories about clients, prospects, referral sources, etc., helps others and helps you with more connections.)

48

YOUR NETWORLDING PRIMARY CIRCLE PARTNER PROFILE
(Use 1 per circle partner)

Name: Primary Phone: Primary Email:

Employed [ ]   Self-employed [ ]   Industry   Title   Employed By:

Current or Former Company's Products and/or Services – Sound Bite: (A quick 30-second overview that defines what you do and how you can help others.)

Personal Professional Skills & Responsibilities – Personal Values: (What you value most in your personal and work relationships?)

Personal Information Affecting Future Decisions – Personal Interests: (What you do you for fun?)

Supporting Others in Networlding – Help Others Connect: (How you can help connect people to those they want to meet or create the opportunities they want to create?)

The kinds of people or opportunities to be connected with – How would you like others to help or support you: (Think about the next 30-60 days as a focus on the support you need.)

Your last great Networlding opportunity you created – The story about how you connected with someone and worked on an opportunity together: (Networlders who share stories about clients, prospects, referral sources, etc., helps others and helps you with more connections.)

YOUR NETWORLDING PRIMARY CIRCLE PARTNER PROFILE
(Use 1 per circle partner)

Name: Primary Phone: Primary Email:

Employed [ ]   Self-employed [ ]   Industry   Title   Employed By:

Current or Former Company's Products and/or Services – Sound Bite: (A quick 30-second overview that defines what you do and how you can help others.)

Personal Professional Skills & Responsibilities – Personal Values: (What you value most in your personal and work relationships?)

Personal Information Affecting Future Decisions – Personal Interests: (What you do you for fun?)

Supporting Others in Networlding – Help Others Connect: (How you can help connect people to those they want to meet or create the opportunities they want to create?)

The kinds of people or opportunities to be connected with – How would you like others to help or support you: (Think about the next 30-60 days as a focus on the support you need.)

Your last great Networlding opportunity you created – The story about how you connected with someone and worked on an opportunity together: (Networlders who share stories about clients, prospects, referral sources, etc., helps others and helps you with more connections.)

YOUR NETWORLDING PRIMARY CIRCLE PARTNER PROFILE

(Use 1 per circle partner)

Name: Primary Phone: Primary Email:

Employed [ ]   Self-employed [ ]   Industry   Title   Employed By:

Current or Former Company's Products and/or Services – Sound Bite: (A quick 30-second overview that defines what you do and how you can help others.)

Personal Professional Skills & Responsibilities – Personal Values: (What you value most in your personal and work relationships?)

Personal Information Affecting Future Decisions – Personal Interests: (What you do you for fun?)

Supporting Others in Networlding – Help Others Connect: (How you can help connect people to those they want to meet or create the opportunities they want to create?)

The kinds of people or opportunities to be connected with – How would you like others to help or support you: (Think about the next 30-60 days as a focus on the support you need.)

Your last great Networlding opportunity you created – The story about how you connected with someone and worked on an opportunity together: (Networlders who share stories about clients, prospects, referral sources, etc., helps others and helps you with more connections.)

51

YOUR NETWORLDING PRIMARY CIRCLE PARTNER PROFILE

(Use 1 per circle partner)

Name: Primary Phone: Primary Email:

Employed [ ]   Self-employed [ ]   Industry   Title   Employed By:

Current or Former Company's Products and/or Services – Sound Bite: (A quick 30-second overview that defines what you do and how you can help others.)

Personal Professional Skills & Responsibilities – Personal Values: (What you value most in your personal and work relationships?)

Personal Information Affecting Future Decisions – Personal Interests: (What you do you for fun?)

Supporting Others in Networlding – Help Others Connect: (How you can help connect people to those they want to meet or create the opportunities they want to create?)

The kinds of people or opportunities to be connected with – How would you like others to help or support you: (Think about the next 30-60 days as a focus on the support you need.)

Your last great Networlding opportunity you created – The story about how you connected with someone and worked on an opportunity together: (Networlders who share stories about clients, prospects, referral sources, etc., helps others and helps you with more connections.)

YOUR NETWORLDING PRIMARY CIRCLE PARTNER PROFILE
(Use 1 per circle partner)

Name: Primary Phone: Primary Email:

Employed [ ]   Self-employed [ ]   Industry   Title   Employed By:

Current or Former Company's Products and/or Services – Sound Bite: (A quick 30-second overview that defines what you do and how you can help others.)

Personal Professional Skills & Responsibilities – Personal Values: (What you value most in your personal and work relationships?)

Personal Information Affecting Future Decisions – Personal Interests: (What you do you for fun?)

Supporting Others in Networlding – Help Others Connect: (How you can help connect people to those they want to meet or create the opportunities they want to create?)

The kinds of people or opportunities to be connected with – How would you like others to help or support you: (Think about the next 30-60 days as a focus on the support you need.)

Your last great Networlding opportunity you created – The story about how you connected with someone and worked on an opportunity together: (Networlders who share stories about clients, prospects, referral sources, etc., helps others and helps you with more connections.)

WHERE TO MEET TOP NETWORLDERS

Where to Meet the Power Elite from *Inc. Magazine's* article by Tahl Raz, "The 10 Secrets of a Master Networker."

Keith Ferrazzi's favorite places to hang with other people on the rise.

Young Presidents' Organization (YPO). The organization is for executive managers under the age of 44 and has regional chapters across the United States.

Political fund-raisers. Although Ferrazzi once ran for office as a Republican, he no longer openly discusses his political affiliation. Why? So he can have access to both parties. He does 3 to 10 fund-raisers at home each year, supporting both regional and national politicians. It's easy pickings at the nexus of money and passion.

Conferences. "Have something unique to say and become a speaker" is Ferrazzi's hard-and-fast rule on attending business conferences. Networking is never easier than when people are coming to you.

Davos World Economic Forum. Held at the end of January or beginning of February each year, Davos is where corporate chieftains and political heavies discuss making the world better while slaloming the Alps. Your best chance of being invited is if you run a multinational or know someone who does. Many of Ferrazzi's most important relationships—including Nike's Phil Knight—have come from Davos.

Nonprofit boards. Ferrazzi suggests starting out by finding four or five issues that are important to you and then supporting them locally. Eventually, the goal is to become a board member.

Renaissance Weekend. Bill Clinton's favorite New Year's event (and, not surprisingly, the place that generated quite a few political appointments) is arguably the network of networks. If you're not a celebrity, a politician, or a friend of a friend, tough luck. This party, held in Charleston, S.C., is invitation only.

Any airplane's first-class cabin. First class is where the bigwigs sit when they fly. When Ferrazzi was at Deloitte Consulting, he'd pay for his own upgrades, and he eventually generated enough business to get the company to pay his way. There's a trick, however, to making it work. "You've got one shot at starting a conversation," he says, "and that's when someone is eating. They're bored and more receptive than at any time during the flight."

TED Conferences. This annual gathering in February in Monterey, Calif., brings together the well-connected nerd set under the theme "Technology, Entertainment, and Design." It's not hard to get an invitation, and the players come out for the heavy mingling, deal making, and often-interesting, if esoteric, seminars.

Allen & Co.'s Conference. New York investment banker Herb Allen organized the first event in 1983 to bring media moguls together at a lush ski resort in Sun Valley, Idaho, to do one thing: make deals. Very big deals.

Networlding Lexicon

Networlding is a seven-step process that helps you build trusting, satisfying and empowering relationships faster. Leaders growing their organizations, businesses or careers experience the creation of transformational opportunities.

Community Circles, Circles, Power-of-Ten Circles, Core Circles, Community Learning Circles, Career Learning Circles	Power-of-Ten Circles are practice Circles of ten or fewer people who gather to learn and practice the seven steps of Networlding. These Circles can be created by you or with support from those continuously signing up to join Networlding Circles all over the world.
Creating a Values Foundation	To get on the path toward establishing your values foundation, take these six actions 1. Decide what matters to you most 2. Identify your values priorities 3. Align your values with your actions 4. Create a personal charter 5. Set goals 6. Establish a one-year plan
Create a Personal Charter	A charter is your mandate to act, an overarching statement that describes who you want to be, what you want to do, the profession or principle to which you want to dedicate your life, and the legacy you want to leave.
Discernment	The key to understanding Networlding Connections. It is a meaningful connection based on an assessment of a potential relationship based on what is exchanged.
Horizon of Observability	The expanded focus of identifying your contacts holistically. This is the foreseeable number of people connected to those whom you meet.
Influencers	Those people of your primary Circle who have the ability to influence other people and their actions. It is not a passive or titled-based concept, at least in the Networld sense.
Influential Networlders	The kinds of behavior exhibited by networlders that might not be automatically associated with people of influence. > Willingness to Give > Community Involvement > Awareness of Other's Needs and Interests > Dependability > Persistence > Covisioning

| **"Learning Circle"** | In a "Learning Circle" you focus on Networlding as a seven-step process that helps build trusting, satisfying and empowering relationships faster. Leaders growing their organizations, businesses, individuals in job search or career transition can focus on a "Learning Circle" experience to create the transformational opportunities. This happens through an exclusive Exchange Support Model. |

| **Networlding** | Networlding is, at its heart, a fun experience. People talk about their unique personal passions. That's what gets us up every morning. We also find most of the groups turn into friendship Circles. They end up setting up picnics, parties and special outings. We are also adding a Networlding Dinners where Networlding members get the change to experience community and create new opportunities for their careers and businesses at the same time. |

| **Networlders' Beliefs** | Although networlders' values are often different, their beliefs are usually similar. They create a "community of faith," people who adhere to the same tenets of success, purpose, and process. |

| **Networlding Beliefs** | The beliefs that evolve over time which provide links to other networlders. They will inspire and motivate you, helping you move towards your goals. They are:
> Anything is possible with the support of others.
> It is important to make a difference.
> You get what you ask for.
> All resources will be provided to reach your goals.
> Life is filled with abundance and opportunities.
> There must be mutual rewards for partners. |

| **Networlding Traits** | The following traits to help identify a good networlder as well as to help you become familiar with the traits you need to develop in yourself. The traits are:
> Supportive
> Continuous Communicators
> Reliable and Responsible
> Influential
> Knowledgeable
> Active Listener
> Empathic
> Appreciative
> Connection-Conscious |

| **Power-of-Ten Extended Circle** | Once you join Networlding your Networlding Power-of-Ten Extended Circle is created after going through the Networlding "Learning Steps." After the five sessions and from any other Circles you choose to join at no extra charge. |

Primary Circle	The Circle that you interact with the most frequently. They are the combination personal think tank and pit team, offering encouragement, information and ideas in achieving what is most important to you. They are members who share traits of networlders, share your values and are influencers.
Structured Exchange	Extensive studies on human networks show that you achieve better results (more connections, ongoing creativity, better opportunities) when you have regular (at least monthly) communications (we call them Exchanges) with a small, diverse group of people. Through the Power-of-Ten Circles, we will show you how to build a powerful Circle of people who can bring new and fresh perspectives to your business or career growth and for whom you can do the same.
Support Exchange Model	The model illustrates the hierarchy of the development of relationships (like Maslow's Hierarchy of Needs for individuals) that evolves from a conscious communication exchange process with a select group of people.

Emotional Support: The part of consciousness that involves feelings. Our feelings about others serve as the foundations for our relationships. The focus of exchanging emotional support with another is to create rapport, a relationship of mutual trust and affinity.

Information Support: Information is a combination of messages. Once there is an initial rapport built, we then feel comfortable to share information of value.

Knowledge Support: Here, we add the element of experience. By sharing our personal experiences and those experiences of others we have heard, we add an additional value to our exchanges with others.

Promotional Support: As we continue to build rapport we naturally share with others the attributes of those whom we value. We heighten the awareness of these Networlding partners to others and in doing so, better position them opportunities that arise.

Wisdom Support: Wisdom adds an element of time, clarity and understanding to our communications with others. Wisdom also adds the element of caring and compassion—a real desire to help others develop and achieve their life's dreams.

Transformational Opportunities: A natural result of emotional, informational, knowledge, promotional and wisdom support is a favorable or advantageous combination of circumstances. Opportunities can be leads or referrals or new jobs or business, personal or professional. The Networlding Exchange creates opportunities we can actually see evolving.

Community: This support results from a series of exchanges. A critical mass is reached when two or more people consciously connect regularly to support one another. There is a ripple effect that occurs as each party to a Networlding relationship shares various forms of support with others in his or her community and it is further shared and so on and so on. If you change yourselves, you will, in turn, change everyone around you and they will in turn, change everyone around them. Eventually, there will be no one in a community not touched. Something changes in the whole matrix of experience.

Fulfillment: A deep, personal sense of satisfaction comes from finding your purpose and making things happen in life that fulfills that purpose. Throughout the Networlding process we receive fulfillment from our exchanges individually and even greater satisfaction from the awareness that we are making a difference for the people we are benefiting through our exchanges. Fulfillment offers us a panoramic view of the literally thousands of conversations we have with others throughout our lifetime and gives us a gauge that measures the degree of satisfaction we feel we are achieving. Celebrating small successes is a big part of this.

(The) Seven Steps of Networlding

1. Establish a Values-Rich Foundation. Identify your top values. Discover linkages to company values and goals.
2. Make Connections for Your Primary. Circle Identify who is currently in your Primary Circle and why.
3. Expand Your Circles. Identify and connect with new people who have similar and complimentary values.
4. Initiate Exchanging Relationships. Develop relationships more effectively by finding out what matters to others.
5. Grow and Nurture Relationships. Develop relationships with Primary Networlding Partners using The Networlding Support Exchange Model.
6. Co-create Opportunities. Create transformational opportunities through continuous exchanges.
7. Recreate Your Networld. Achieve your goals: constantly reassess and expand relationships that align with your values

MY NETWORLDING ACTION PLAN - MONTH OF JANUARY

What are the results I have achieved to date on my goal?

Changes to goal (if applicable):

What top benefits have I received from your Primary Circle Partners this month?

What top benefits have I offered my Primary Circle Partners this month?

Partners supported:	What did I give:
	What did I receive:
Great organizations or trade shows I have attended:	Details of events. Top people whom you met and will follow up with, etc.:
Organizations I plan to join:	Special committees, events or people:
Great referrals I have received:	Details:

Great potential partners who might become
Primary Circle Partners:

Scheduled meetings and conversations I will initiate:

Partners I will follow-up with in the next month:

Ideas for support I can offer in the
future and support I can request:

Partners I plan to co-create opportunities within
the next month:

Ideas for co-creating with these partners:

Top partnering story:

Overall estimated financial results from connections:

Breakdown of results:

To Do's:

MY NETWORLDING ACTION PLAN - MONTH OF FEBRUARY

What are the results I have achieved to date on my goal?

Changes to goal (if applicable):

What top benefits have I received from your Primary Circle Partners this month?

What top benefits have I offered my Primary Circle Partners this month?

Partners supported:	What did I give:
	What did I receive:
Great organizations or trade shows I have attended:	Details of events. Top people whom you met and will follow up with, etc.:
Organizations I plan to join:	Special committees, events or people:
Great referrals I have received:	Details:

Great potential partners who might become Primary Circle Partners:

Scheduled meetings and conversations I will initiate:

Partners I will follow-up with in the next month:

Ideas for support I can offer in the future and support I can request:

Partners I plan to co-create opportunities within the next month:

Ideas for co-creating with these partners:

Top partnering story:

Overall estimated financial results from connections:

Breakdown of results:

To Do's:

MY NETWORLDING ACTION PLAN - MONTH OF MARCH

What are the results I have achieved to date on my goal?

Changes to goal (if applicable):

What top benefits have I received from your Primary Circle Partners this month?

What top benefits have I offered my Primary Circle Partners this month?

Partners supported:	What did I give:
	What did I receive:
Great organizations or trade shows I have attended:	Details of events. Top people whom you met and will follow up with, etc.:
Organizations I plan to join:	Special committees, events or people:
Great referrals I have received:	Details:

63

Great potential partners who might become
Primary Circle Partners:

Scheduled meetings and conversations I will initiate:

Partners I will follow-up with in the next month:

Ideas for support I can offer in the
future and support I can request:

Partners I plan to co-create opportunities within
the next month:

Ideas for co-creating with these partners:

Top partnering story:

Overall estimated financial results from connections:

Breakdown of results:

To Do's:

MY NETWORLDING ACTION PLAN - MONTH OF APRIL

What are the results I have achieved to date on my goal?

Changes to goal (if applicable):

What top benefits have I received from your Primary Circle Partners this month?

What top benefits have I offered my Primary Circle Partners this month?

Partners supported:	What did I give:
	What did I receive:
Great organizations or trade shows I have attended:	Details of events. Top people whom you met and will follow up with, etc.:
Organizations I plan to join:	Special committees, events or people:
Great referrals I have received:	Details:

Great potential partners who might become
Primary Circle Partners:

Scheduled meetings and conversations I will initiate:

Partners I will follow-up with in the next month:

Ideas for support I can offer in the
future and support I can request:

Partners I plan to co-create opportunities within
the next month:

Ideas for co-creating with these partners:

Top partnering story:

Overall estimated financial results from connections:

Breakdown of results:

To Do's:

66

MY NETWORLDING ACTION PLAN - MONTH OF MAY

What are the results I have achieved to date on my goal?

Changes to goal (if applicable):

What top benefits have I received from your Primary Circle Partners this month?

What top benefits have I offered my Primary Circle Partners this month?

Partners supported:	What did I give:
	What did I receive:
Great organizations or trade shows I have attended:	Details of events. Top people whom you met and will follow up with, etc.:
Organizations I plan to join:	Special committees, events or people:
Great referrals I have received:	Details:

Great potential partners who might become Primary Circle Partners:

Scheduled meetings and conversations I will initiate:

Partners I will follow-up with in the next month:

Ideas for support I can offer in the future and support I can request:

Partners I plan to co-create opportunities within the next month:

Ideas for co-creating with these partners:

Top partnering story:

Overall estimated financial results from connections:

Breakdown of results:

To Do's:

MY NETWORLDING ACTION PLAN - MONTH OF JUNE

What are the results I have achieved to date on my goal?

Changes to goal (if applicable):

What top benefits have I received from your Primary Circle Partners this month?

What top benefits have I offered my Primary Circle Partners this month?

Partners supported:	What did I give:
	What did I receive:
Great organizations or trade shows I have attended:	Details of events. Top people whom you met and will follow up with, etc.:
Organizations I plan to join:	Special committees, events or people:
Great referrals I have received:	Details:

69

Great potential partners who might become Primary Circle Partners:

Scheduled meetings and conversations I will initiate:

Partners I will follow-up with in the next month:

Ideas for support I can offer in the future and support I can request:

Partners I plan to co-create opportunities within the next month:

Ideas for co-creating with these partners:

Top partnering story:

Overall estimated financial results from connections:

Breakdown of results:

To Do's:

MY NETWORLDING ACTION PLAN - MONTH OF JULY

What are the results I have achieved to date on my goal?

Changes to goal (if applicable):

What top benefits have I received from your Primary Circle Partners this month?

What top benefits have I offered my Primary Circle Partners this month?

Partners supported:	What did I give:
	What did I receive:
Great organizations or trade shows I have attended:	Details of events. Top people whom you met and will follow up with, etc.:
Organizations I plan to join:	Special committees, events or people:
Great referrals I have received:	Details:

71

Great potential partners who might become Primary Circle Partners:

Scheduled meetings and conversations I will initiate:

Partners I will follow-up with in the next month:

Ideas for support I can offer in the future and support I can request:

Partners I plan to co-create opportunities within the next month:

Ideas for co-creating with these partners:

Top partnering story:

Overall estimated financial results from connections:

Breakdown of results:

To Do's:

MY NETWORLDING ACTION PLAN - MONTH OF AUGUST

What are the results I have achieved to date on my goal?

Changes to goal (if applicable):

What top benefits have I received from your Primary Circle Partners this month?

What top benefits have I offered my Primary Circle Partners this month?

Partners supported:	What did I give:
	What did I receive:
Great organizations or trade shows I have attended:	Details of events. Top people whom you met and will follow up with, etc.:
Organizations I plan to join:	Special committees, events or people:
Great referrals I have received:	Details:

73

Great potential partners who might become
Primary Circle Partners:

Scheduled meetings and conversations I will initiate:

Partners I will follow-up with in the next month:

Ideas for support I can offer in the
future and support I can request:

Partners I plan to co-create opportunities within
the next month:

Ideas for co-creating with these partners:

Top partnering story:

Overall estimated financial results from connections:

Breakdown of results:

To Do's:

MY NETWORLDING ACTION PLAN - MONTH OF SEPTEMBER

What are the results I have achieved to date on my goal?

Changes to goal (if applicable):

What top benefits have I received from your Primary Circle Partners this month?

What top benefits have I offered my Primary Circle Partners this month?

Partners supported:	What did I give:
	What did I receive:
Great organizations or trade shows I have attended:	Details of events. Top people whom you met and will follow up with, etc.:
Organizations I plan to join:	Special committees, events or people:
Great referrals I have received:	Details:

Great potential partners who might become Primary Circle Partners:

Scheduled meetings and conversations I will initiate:

Partners I will follow-up with in the next month:

Ideas for support I can offer in the future and support I can request:

Partners I plan to co-create opportunities within the next month:

Ideas for co-creating with these partners:

Top partnering story:

Overall estimated financial results from connections:

Breakdown of results:

To Do's:

MY NETWORLDING ACTION PLAN - MONTH OF OCTOBER

What are the results I have achieved to date on my goal?

Changes to goal (if applicable):

What top benefits have I received from your Primary Circle Partners this month?

What top benefits have I offered my Primary Circle Partners this month?

Partners supported:	What did I give:
	What did I receive:
Great organizations or trade shows I have attended:	Details of events. Top people whom you met and will follow up with, etc.:
Organizations I plan to join:	Special committees, events or people:
Great referrals I have received:	Details:

Great potential partners who might become Primary Circle Partners:

Scheduled meetings and conversations I will initiate:

Partners I will follow-up with in the next month:

Ideas for support I can offer in the future and support I can request:

Partners I plan to co-create opportunities within the next month:

Ideas for co-creating with these partners:

Top partnering story:

Overall estimated financial results from connections:

Breakdown of results:

To Do's:

MY NETWORLDING ACTION PLAN - MONTH OF NOVEMBER

What are the results I have achieved to date on my goal?

Changes to goal (if applicable):

What top benefits have I received from your Primary Circle Partners this month?

What top benefits have I offered my Primary Circle Partners this month?

Partners supported:	What did I give:
	What did I receive:
Great organizations or trade shows I have attended:	Details of events. Top people whom you met and will follow up with, etc.:
Organizations I plan to join:	Special committees, events or people:
Great referrals I have received:	Details:

79

Great potential partners who might become Primary Circle Partners:

Scheduled meetings and conversations I will initiate:

Partners I will follow-up with in the next month:

Ideas for support I can offer in the future and support I can request:

Partners I plan to co-create opportunities within the next month:

Ideas for co-creating with these partners:

Top partnering story:

Overall estimated financial results from connections:

Breakdown of results:

To Do's:

MY NETWORLDING ACTION PLAN - MONTH OF DECEMBER

What are the results I have achieved to date on my goal?

Changes to goal (if applicable):

What top benefits have I received from your Primary Circle Partners this month?

What top benefits have I offered my Primary Circle Partners this month?

Partners supported:	What did I give:
	What did I receive:
Great organizations or trade shows I have attended:	Details of events. Top people whom you met and will follow up with, etc.:
Organizations I plan to join:	Special committees, events or people:
Great referrals I have received:	Details:

81

Great potential partners who might become Primary Circle Partners:

Scheduled meetings and conversations I will initiate:

Partners I will follow-up with in the next month:

Ideas for support I can offer in the future and support I can request:

Partners I plan to co-create opportunities within the next month:

Ideas for co-creating with these partners:

Top partnering story:

Overall estimated financial results from connections:

Breakdown of results:

To Do's:

Networlding Guidelines

- Realize that Networlding is about creating communities of support, built on trust, respect and well-being. It's a process of collaboration that achieves mutual goals and leads to professional and personal fulfillment. This is distinct from what many people consider "networking." For many, traditional networking is transactional – as in "what can you do for me?" That's why traditional networking seems unsatisfying, empty to some.

- With Networlding, create authentic relationships and alliances with others that share your values. Create partners in what you want to accomplish, as you partner with others in fulfilling their goals.

- Make a connection. Develop rapport, chemistry first.

- Be yourself. Be authentic. Maintain eye contact. Be present with others — in person and on the phone.

- Listen more than you talk. Real listening is a gift. Be curious. Be an active listener. Ask questions, but don't interrogate. Focus your attention on the person you have met. Learn about this person, and look for ways to support him or her — with information, acknowledgement or other support. If this person is a giver, he or she will naturally want to return the favor.

- Be a giver and identify givers as you Networld. — Avoid takers. Givers care about you and about creating an even exchange; takers talk only about themselves and have little interest in you.

- Think exchange. Like any healthy relationship, a Networlding relationship is based on mutual exchange and benefit.

- Give first, and establish trust before you ask for something for yourself.

- Clarify your own values. Notice how others express their values, beyond what they may tell you. This is a critical time saver.

- Make it easy for others to understand how people benefit from working with you. Develop a simple way to authentically share the difference you make in the lives of others.

- Keep your word. Follow up with others if you said you would, and take and return calls if you agreed to talk later. Realize that as you Networld, you are also building your identity in your organization and the community.

- Honor time constraints of others. When you contact someone you have met or would like to know, find out if it's a good time to talk. If someone tells you he has ten minutes to talk, complete the conversation in less than ten minutes, or offer to speak later when it's more conducive to have a conversation. People will really appreciate this!

- Make appropriate requests. This is a crucial area of Networlding. If you ask too much too soon, you shut down the relationship. Making requests is an art that can make an enormous difference in your identity.

- As you develop Networlding relationships, there will be an ebb and flow as to who is supporting who. Be attentive. A good Networlding relationship is empowering, energizing. Notice those relationships that are not.

- Developing powerful relationships takes time. The investment is worth it. Learn to Networld successfully and change your life.

Networlding Action Plan Ideas

Some of the following ideas can be written into your Networlding Action Plan. Go through the list and highlight 4-5 development ideas that resonate with you. Use them for development planning. Re-read the list or a portion of it occasionally to remind you to focus on a healthy balance.

- Join new professional/trade organizations to broaden your network.

- Read the Wall Street Journal every day.

- Volunteer for a non-profit organization on a committee which serves an entirely different function than you work in daily.

- Meet with a different "expert/influencer" every month for breakfast, lunch or after work to discuss their journey to success.

- Meet with an accomplished person (accomplished in a quality/areas that you would like to develop) every month to discuss how they developed those skills.

- Offer to serve as an officer, board member or speaker/presenter for professional organizations.

- Work on a company team/committee in an area of the organization in which you are interested (either functionally or operationally). Ask questions; build relationships.

- Register for a training module that would enhance some of your top competencies.

- Take a course unrelated to anything you do or in a skill you would like to develop and think about how you could utilize that new skill in your work.

- Redesign your work and/or your work team based on your values and mission; trade some responsibilities with others on your team.

- Record positives that happen in your journal--values that are evident in others' behavior.

- Realistically assess your strengths and weaknesses, both personally and professionally. Use a 360-degree assessment tool to get others' honest feedback and take action on their perceptions.

- Take a Myers-Briggs Personality Type Indicator (MBTI) to determine your personality preferences and how to communicate with those different from yourself.

- "Job Shadow" a person for a workday to determine your interest in that type of position. Make a list of what you really enjoyed and what you did not.

- Explore why a past project did not work with trusted colleagues to provide new perspectives to your vision.

- When launching a new project, get to know and get input from the people who will enable your project to work. Obtain their buy-in by incorporating their ideas into the project.

- Find an "expert" player in your profession with whom you can Networld. Think of the kinds of support you can exchange.

- Hire a coach who will work with you as your partner.

- Continue to step back and assess your progress. What has gone well? What needs improvement? Are you accomplishing your original goal? Does your original goal need to grow or shift?

- Think about times in your business and in your personal life when you were "in the zone" (really excited and energized.) What were you doing at that time? Find ways to incorporate more of that into your life.

- Describe what you really want to accomplish in concrete terms. What does success look like – what will you be doing? How is that different from now? What can you do to move in that direction today? Describe what the specific rewards will be.

- Think about your goals and values. Make sure they all belong to you. Are you doing anything because you think you are supposed to, because you think you should or because you want to? If it is a should do, eliminate it or restate it positively.

- Give yourself time off to see what new ideas appear.

- List the 5-7 most important tasks for the day. Arrange them in reverse order of ease of completing. Do the most difficult task first and the rest of the day will be easier.

- Try totally new leisure activities.

- Find foods that give you energy.

- Ensure that you have enough light.

- Surround yourself with a supportive community and allow time for volunteer activities.

- Read inspirational books.

- Add variety to your day.

- Use your lunch as a real break and meet with someone you enjoy.

- Eliminate clutter so you can eliminate distractions and energy drains. Create space for new opportunities.

- Find a player or coach in function that you're interested in, different from your current function.

- Give yourself time for innovation and creativity.

- Be kind to yourself. Those critical voices impede the process; let them go.

- Interview a colleague to discuss how they incorporate their values and interests into their job. Think about how you can do this, too.

- Continue to update and enhance your computer, Internet, other important-to-the-world technology skills.

- Challenges provide us the greatest opportunity for learning. Incorporate new projects into your current work to upgrade your skills, increase your knowledge or utilize and expand your creativity.

- Network and interview benchmarks to keep current on industry/business/profession trends; to help you forecast and plan new practices required for the future.

- Know that you have choices.

- Take time each day for pure pleasure.

- Move laterally to broaden a skill set.

- Take a 360-degree assessment to identify how your boss, your peer/colleagues and your direct reports (if you have them) assesses your strengths. Clarify their feedback and then incorporate some of this info into your development plan.

- Check your action plan progress and modify or accelerate on the first or last working day of every month (write in an appointment on your calendar.)

- Get involved in enough other areas of your life to enhance your feelings of competence even when one area is going wrong.

- Identify an issue that has gone unresolved (within your line of sight,) assemble the right team and solve it.

- Continue to grow and dream. Explore your niche. And when you're ready, create a new one.

- Become an early adopter of trends, products and services.

For specific competency-based development suggestions, we recommend the following resources:

1. Successful Manager's Handbook, PDI, International (612-339-0927, www.pdi-corp.com)
2. Successful Executive's Handbook, PDI, International (MPG Resource Guide, Blessing-White (800-222-1349, www.blessingwhite.com)

Networlding Bibliography

***Achieving Success Through Social Capital**: Tapping Hidden Resources in Your Personal and Business Networks* by Wayne E. Baker, (Hardcover - 144 pages John Wiley & Sons; ISBN: 0787953091)

***In Good Company**: How Social Capital Makes Organizations Work* by Don Cohen, (Laurence Prusak, Hardcover - 224 pages Harvard Business School Pr; ISBN: 087584913X)

Fifty-Two Ways to Reconnect, Follow-Up and Stay in Touch, When You Don't Have Time to Network by Anne Baber, Lynne Waymon, (Paperback, Waymon & Associates; ISBN:0840392244)

Knowledge and Social Capital, Foundations and Applications by Eric L. Lesser (Editor), Paperback - 304 pages, Butterworth-Heinemann Ltd; ISBN: 0750672226

***Networking Smart**: How to Build Relationships for Personal and Organizational Success* by Wayne E. Baker, Paperback - 400 pages, iUniverse.com; ISBN: 0595007864

***Networlding**: Building Relationships and Opportunities for Success* by Melissa Giovagnoli, Jocelyn Carter-Miller, (Hardcover - 216 pages 1st edition, Jossey-Bass; ISBN: 0787948195)

***The Power of Two**: How Companies of All Sizes Can Build Alliance Networks That Generate Business Opportunities* (Jossey-Bass Business & Management Series, by John K. Conlon, Melissa Giovagnoli, (Hardcover - 256 pages Jossey-Bass; ISBN: 0787909467)

***Power Networking**: Using the Contacts You Don't Even Know You Have to Succeed in the Job You Want* by Marc Kramer, (Paperback - 160 pages NTC Publ Group; ISBN: 0844244945)

Networlding Reflections

1/ "Wisdom begins in wonder." – *Socrates*

2/ "When we go outside of ourselves and focus on others' needs, we expend our energy in caring, as opposed to acting out of fear." —*Anonymous*

3/ "You are not here merely to make a living. You are here to enable the world to live more amply, with greater vision, with a finer spirit of hope and achievement. You are here to enrich the world, and you impoverish yourself if you forget the errand." – *Woodrow Wilson*

4/ "In environments in which human needs are acknowledged and talent and creativity are allowed to flourish, employees give their all." —*Charles Garfield*

5/ "All the companies that are alive are realizing that they need more creative, vital, and adaptable workers."—*David Whyte*

6/ "Your ultimate goal in life is to become your best self. Your immediate goal is to get on the path that will lead you there. Why should you feel guilty if you refuse to be intimidated by [someone] who persists in standing in the way of your being the best self or who is "hurt" when you finally manage it?—*David Viscott, M.D.*

7/ The highest love a person can have for you is to wish for you to evolve into the best person you can be. No one owns you, no matter what your relationship. You are not here on this earth to fulfill the unmet dreams of a frustrated parent or to protect another person from facing the reality of himself or the world. You are here to develop and grow, to do your share to make the outside world in which you live, the world that is you, as honest and as true to your feelings as you possibly can." —*David Viscott, M.D.*

8/ "Prosperity is living easily and happily in the real world, whether you have money or not."—*Jerry Gillies*

9/ "Leadership is authentic self-expression that creates value."—*Kevin Cashman*

10/ "Those who think the world is a dark place are blind to the light that might illuminate their lives."—*Wayne Dyer*

11/ "Every man must be his own leader. He now knows enough not to follow other people. He must follow the light that's within himself, and through this light he will create a new community."—*Laurens Van Der Post*

12/ "Work is the very fire where we are baked to perfection, and like the master of the fire itself, we add the essential ingredient and fulfillment when we walk into the flames ourselves."—*David Whyte*

13/ "Trust is our trail guide through the wilderness of change." —*Bill McCarthy*

14/ "The opposite of trusting in the unexpected is trying to control the uncontrollable– clearly an impossible task."—*Angeles Arrien*

15/ "Life's most urgent question is, 'What are you doing for others?'" —*Martin Luther King, Jr.*

16/ "The companies that create the most nourishing environments for personal growth will attract the most talented people."—*John Naisbitt*

17/ "You must do the thing you think you cannot do."—*Eleanor Roosevelt*

18/ "You must be the change you wish to see in the world." —*Mahatma Mohandas Gandhi*

19/ "The choice we offer people is what creates accountability."—*Peter Block*

20/ "Work can provide the opportunity for spiritual and personal, as well as financial, growth. If it doesn't, then we're wasting far too much of our lives on it." —*James Autry*

21/ "Try not to become a man of success, but rather try to become a man of value." —*Albert Einstein*

5 Rules for Networking into Organizations

1/ Leverage the corporate grapevine. Every company has one. It is not formal but still, according to management consulting experts like Drucker and Peters, is the real power in an organization. The grapevine is made up of certain individuals who have the ability to influence more than others. These people might be at the top of the company or somewhere climbing toward the top. They exhibit great skills of communication.

They know how to get things done quickly and at the same time, grow even stronger professional friend ships. They can be at the top of an organization, in line management or not. The best networkers are "connectors" who will connect you with others for mutual gain. Ask your network who they think these "connectors" are at an organization you are targeting and then ask to be introduced to them. Set up regular calls with connectors and share support for one another. You will find "connectors" are the best networking partners.

2/ Become a connector. Learn the skills of the connector. Practice developing these skills by writing down the names of a couple of people you would like to become more connected with and then think of people they might like to meet that you know. When you call them or meet with "connectors," have people in mind that you think they should meet. With this strategy you become a "connector" and will be sought after by other "connectors."

Think of different types of connections you can make (e.g. helping people locate new products or services, helping them find new information or gain insights on new and better processes.) For example, someone you know may have had experience in a field that someone you want to meet might benefit from. By introducing these people to each other, you add value through the connection. You build trust and credibility throughout your network as you connect one great person to another.

3/ Grow your curiosity. Great networkers are curious. They continually wonder what is going on at organiza tions they are targeting. Ask yourself questions like, "What can I be doing this week to find out more valu able insights on the key organizations I am targeting?" Survey your network with questions as to insights they have about this organization. Ask your network to explore with their connections what they might know about your targeted organizations. You will gather a great amount of information quickly with this process.

4/ Build a network of exchangers. One of the biggest problems to growing relationships is removing the fear people have around sharing or exchanging information, knowledge, connections and opportunities. Many think that if they share too much they will experience a loss of power. But consider this, if everyone is hoarding knowledge and let's say only five people are sharing, then aren't those five people five times more knowledgeable than the rest? They actually have more collective knowledge and as a result, can make more informed decisions faster, which of course, is the name of the game in this New Network Economy.

5/ Know it's all about the people. It might sound incredibly simple but when you shift from thinking about the company you are targeting to thinking about the people, and especially the "connectors" in the company, you focus on where the power lies in this new economy. Everything starts and ends with people—certain people who are ready, willing and able to connect and leverage their collective knowledge. The rule be comes in this new economy, "He or she who shares the fastest, the best and the most often, wins." Find the right connections and you get the greatest return on your investment of time. It's all about finding and developing relationships with the right people.

10 Questions to Ask Yourself to Create Top Performing Networks

"Leaders have people who play to their strengths and people who cover their weaknesses."
—Bruce McNicol, Ascent of a Leader

1/ Who in your network will play to your strengths?

2/ Who will cover your weaknesses?

3/ What one person would you like to meet if you could network with anyone in the world? What qualities does that person have? List them and then look for people who have similar qualities.

4/ What top three industry leaders does your network listen to the most?

5/ What top three leaders in all other industries do they most admire?

6/ What if the network you had comprised of only top performers? What qualities would they have? What qualities do you have to would complement theirs?

7/ How can you listen better every day? Top-performing networkers are top listeners.

8/ Who is one person you know who helps others in the organization above and beyond his or her own work responsibilities?

9/ What one thing would you like to be doing or do differently that you are not doing now? (e.g. have great meetings that lead to new business or design a program that comes in under budget and on time.)

10/ What would it look, sound, feel like to be successful in networking in this organization?

Created by Melissa Giovagnoli, Networlding.com– with special contributor to this section, Jackie Sloane of Sloane Communications, Chicago, IL.

10 Questions to Open Up a Conversation and Start Great Business Relationships

The questions below are examples of those you can use to start engaging conversations. Your goal in meeting others is to help them feel at ease and at the same time, generate some conversation that will serve as a springboard for future conversations. You are searching for Points of Commonality (things you share in common) and Points of Credibility (things that make this person unique and valuable to your network.)

1/ What interested you in attending this event?

2/ Is there any person you would like to meet that might be here?

3/ What is one thing you have done this week that has been really exciting to you?

4/ Who is one person you admire most in your industry?

5/ What one talent do you have that makes you most proud in your work?

6/ If you weren't doing what you are doing right now to make a living, what would you be doing?

7/ What one quality matters most to you that people should have to work with you effectively?

8/ When you were ten, what did you want to do with your life?

9/ What one activity did you best perform at in high school?

10/ How is that work you did a part of your life today?

Created by Melissa Giovagnoli, Networlding.com– with special contributor to this section, Jackie Sloane of Sloane Communications, Chicago, IL.

9 Top Networking Myths

1. Anyone can network well. Some people are good at making lots of connections, however, effective networking is about creating quality relationships with people you can count on to collaborate with you developing all kinds of opportunities for each other throughout the course of your professional career.

2. Women and men network the same way. Men tend to focus on opportunities that come out of networking relationships while women tend to focus more on the relationships. Actually men can learn from women and women from men, how to bring these two skills together to create better opportunities faster.

3. Networking is just "partying" in a business environment. Networking opportunities often coincide with social activities in a business setting. Do not take advantage of readily available food and drink by over-indulging in either.

4. Networking does not come naturally to most people. What comes naturally for some, but not many, is the ability to meet and converse with almost anyone. Effective networking, however, goes beyond the ability to "connect" with others. It takes strategic ability to discern what opportunities will be best for each person with whom you network. Every key relationship you choose to develop takes strategizing to determine when, how and what you will focus on to leverage each other's opportunities.

5. Networking is also called the "Old Boys' Network." While the "Old Boys' Networks" utilize many effective net working techniques to get what they want, they are not the embodiment of networking. Networking in its purest form does not involve exclusivity, elitism or secrecy.

6. You can go to a networking event, meet someone and make something happen in a few minutes. Great opportunities can evolve within minutes of an initial networking meeting; however, you cannot force it to happen. You can use meetings to meet great people, but you can't force something to happen. Networking in the '80s and '90s was often focused on doing business or pushing for career connections without first creating connection. Good networkers know that they must first make a connection, then build the relationship, and then explore opportunities for themselves and their partners.

7. Networking is one-dimensional. Effective networking is holistic. It requires us to look at the human being behind the title. Meeting influential people is first about knowing what matters to that person and then, sharing with them how what matters to you complements what matters to him or her. This connection starts a "joint" conversation as to how you can support each other's goals.

8. Good networkers are extroverted. Many good networkers are introverted. They don't enjoy going out to meetings but they do it anyway, deciding that they would rather meet one or two people they can build strong relationships with than not make connections. They realize that growing their careers requires them to build relationships with diverse types of people with whom they can share support for growing successful.

9. Networking is a numbers game. Networking is first and foremost a quality game. It is important to be prepared (success happens when preparation meets opportunity) by knowing what your goals and dreams are and sharing them clearly with the right people. Look for people who are natural networkers whom you admire. They are out there. If you don't know of any, ask a trusted friend for his or her suggestion. Be on the lookout through your local and national industry publications for leaders you admire. Know who these people are. Find out what matters to them. Develop relationships with them by identifying those things they care about that also matters to you. Now you have a springboard to a quality relationship that can last a lifetime, building opportunities for you and those in your network.

Created by Melissa Giovagnoli, Networlding– with special contributor to this section, Dan Limbach, publisher of www.schmoozemonger.

www.ingramcontent.com/pod-product-compliance
Lightning Source LLC
Chambersburg PA
CBHW051228200326
41519CB00025B/7287